PUBLIC FINANCIAL MANAGEMENT SYSTEMS—MYANMAR

KEY ELEMENTS FROM A FINANCIAL MANAGEMENT PERSPECTIVE

MAY 2020

ASIAN DEVELOPMENT BANK

ADB

© 2020 Asian Development Bank
6 ADB Avenue, Mandaluyong City, 1550 Metro Manila, Philippines
Tel +63 2 8632 4444; Fax +63 2 8636 2444
www.adb.org

Some rights reserved. Published in 2020.

ISBN 978-92-9262-225-1 (print), 978-92-9262-226-8 (electronic)
Publication Stock No. TCS200112-2
DOI: http://dx.doi.org/10.22617/ TCS200112-2

The views expressed in this publication are those of the authors and do not necessarily reflect the views and policies of the Asian Development Bank (ADB) or its Board of Governors or the governments they represent.

ADB does not guarantee the accuracy of the data included in this publication and accepts no responsibility for any consequence of their use. The mention of specific companies or products of manufacturers does not imply that they are endorsed or recommended by ADB in preference to others of a similar nature that are not mentioned.

By making any designation of or reference to a particular territory or geographic area, or by using the term "country" in this document, ADB does not intend to make any judgments as to the legal or other status of any territory or area.

Corrigenda to ADB publications may be found at http://www.adb.org/publications/corrigenda.

Notes:
In this publication, "$" refers to United States dollars.

Printed on recycled paper

Contents

Tables, Figures, and Boxes

Acknowledgments

The project team of the Procurement, Portfolio and Financial Management Department of the Asian Development Bank (ADB)—Aman Trana, Director, Public Financial Management Division; Srinivasan Janardanam, Principal Financial Management Specialist; Akmal Nartayev, Senior Financial Management Specialist; and Myra Ravelo, Senior Financial Management Officer—would like to thank the following government officials who met with Nishan Mendis (consultant) and made valuable contributions to this report.

Service Regulation and Financial Regulation Division, Budget Department
Daw San San Nwe, Deputy Director

Foreign Exchange Subdivison, Budget Department
Daw Aye Aye Mon, Deputy Director

State Administrative Organizations, Ministries and Departments Budget Division 1, Ministries and Departments Budget Division 2, State Economic Enterprises (SEE) Budget Division and Intergovernmental Fiscal Relation Division, Budget Department
Daw Theingi Oo, Director
Daw Naw Wilmar Oo, Director
Deputy Directors
Assistant Directors
Director of SEEs
Director of Intergovernmental Fiscal Relation Division

External Debt Section, Treasury Department
Daw Ni Ni Than, Director
Deputy Directors

Project Appraisal and Progress Reporting Department
Daw Ni Ni Lwin, Director

Planning Department
Daw Thwe Thwe Chit, Director General

Foreign Economic Relations Department
Daw Moh Moh Naing, Director, United Nations/International Organizations Section

Office of the Auditor General of the Union
Daw Naing Thet Oo, Director General
Daw Thandar Lay, Director
Deputy Directors

Myanma Economic Bank
Deputy General Manager

Central Bank of Myanmar
U Win Hteik, Director of Foreign Exchange Management
Daw Nwe Ni Tun, Director

Project Management Unit
Daw Zin Zin Htike, Deputy Project Director, Maubin–Pyapon Road Rehabilitation
Project
Daw Khine Zabel Thinn, Accountant Officer, Maubin–Pyapon Road Rehabilitation
Project
Project Management Unit officials, Greater Mekong Subregion East–West
Economic Corridor (GMS EWEC) Eindu–Kawkareik Road Improvement Project

The assistance of the following ADB staff is likewise gratefully acknowledged: Mi Mi
Naing, Associate Project Analyst; Christopher Spohr, Principal Portfolio Management
Specialist; Duy-Thanh Bui, Principal Energy Economist; Soe Mar Thaung, Senior Operations
Assistant; Benylda Urbano, Project Management Specialist and Technical Assistance
Coordinator/Consultant; Aung Tun, National Consultant, Governance; and Yan P. Oo,
former Programs Officer.

Abbreviations

ADB	–	Asian Development Bank
AIMS	–	Aid Information Management System
CPA	–	certified public accountant
CTLA	–	Controller's Department, Loan Administration Division
DAP	–	Development Assistance Policy
DACU	–	Development Assistance Coordination Unit
FERD	–	Foreign Economic Relations Department
GAAP	–	Generally Accepted Accounting Principles
MAC	–	Myanmar Accountancy Council
MEB	–	Myanma Economic Bank
MFRS	–	Myanmar Financial Reporting Standards
MOPF	–	Ministry of Planning and Finance
MYRM	–	Myanmar Resident Mission
OAG	–	Office of the Auditor General
PAC	–	public account committee
PAPRD	–	Project Appraisal and Progress Reporting Department
PFM	–	public financial management
PMU	–	project management unit
ROSC	–	Report on Observance of Standards and Codes
SEE	–	state economic enterprise

Currency Equivalents

Currency unit – kyat (MMK)

MMK1.00 = $-.00070

$1.00 = MMK1,385.06

I.   Introduction

This report is designed to support fiduciary risk assessments of projects financed by the Asian Development Bank (ADB) in the Republic of the Union of Myanmar. It provides information on Myanmar's public financial management (PFM) systems in the areas of funds flow, accounting, auditing, and related matters, and will be particularly useful to project officers who process and implement ADB-funded projects. The information contained in this report may be leveraged when conducting PFM assessments of executing and implementing agencies, as well as when designing PFM arrangements such as disbursements, reporting, and auditing.

II. Key Players

The key players in the PFM system of Myanmar are listed below and illustrated in Figure 1. An outline of the administrative structure of government at the national and subnational level is in Appendix 1.

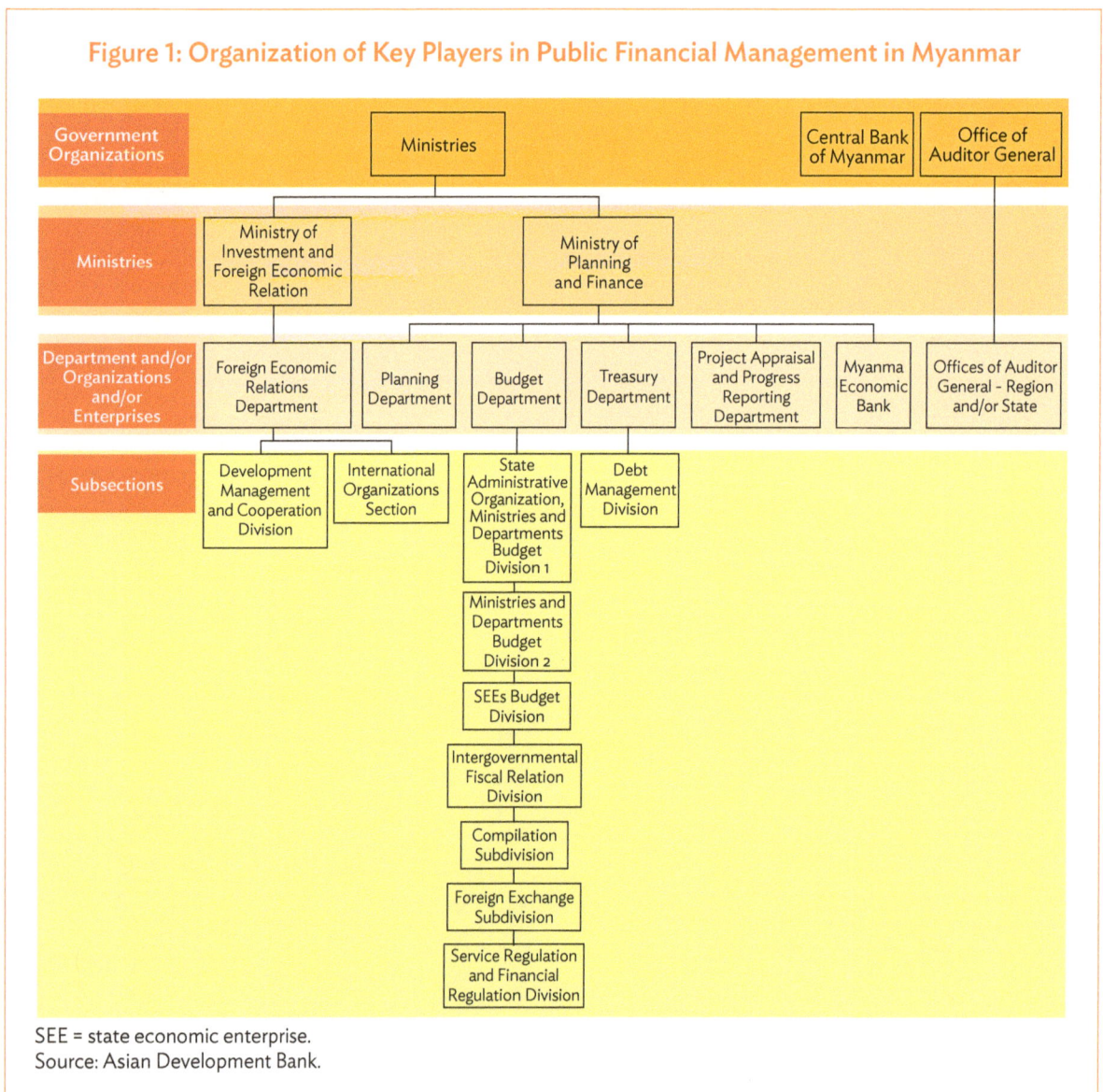

Figure 1: Organization of Key Players in Public Financial Management in Myanmar

Government Organizations	Ministries		Central Bank of Myanmar	Office of Auditor General

Ministries
- Ministry of Investment and Foreign Economic Relation
- Ministry of Planning and Finance

Department and/or Organizations and/or Enterprises
- Foreign Economic Relations Department
- Planning Department
- Budget Department
- Treasury Department
- Project Appraisal and Progress Reporting Department
- Myanma Economic Bank
- Offices of Auditor General - Region and/or State

Subsections
- Development Management and Cooperation Division
- International Organizations Section
- State Administrative Organization, Ministries and Departments Budget Division 1
- Ministries and Departments Budget Division 2
- SEEs Budget Division
- Intergovernmental Fiscal Relation Division
- Compilation Subdivision
- Foreign Exchange Subdivision
- Service Regulation and Financial Regulation Division
- Debt Management Division

SEE = state economic enterprise.
Source: Asian Development Bank.

A. Ministry of Investment and Foreign Economic Relations

Foreign Economic Relations Department

The Foreign Economic Relations Department (FERD) is the coordinating agency and focal point for for bilateral countries, United Nations agencies, and international organizations in mobilizing external resources and development assistance. It aims to promote economic cooperation with foreign countries as well as external organizations for mobilization of external resources in forms of grants, loans, and technical assistance for the economic and social development of the country.[1] FERD also serves as Secretariat to the Development Assistance Coordination Unit (DACU) and supports the DACU by regularly assessing the effectiveness of development assistance, collects, and analyzes development assistance data, and maintains the "Mohinga" Aid Information Management System (AIMS).[2]

B. Ministry of Planning and Finance

Planning Department

The Planning Department of the Ministry of Planning and Finance (MOPF) is responsible for formulation of government's annual short-term and long-term development plans. The department provides required gross domestic product (GDP) data to compile medium-term framework and annual budget estimates. It coordinates with government entities responsible for sector plans and with state and/or regional governments responsible for subnational plans. The department also oversees the preparation of annual investment program (capital budget) and supports the work of the planning commission chaired by the President.

Budget Department

The Budget Department of the MOPF formulates and implements the annual state budget of Myanmar within the country's macroeconomic framework.[3] Its key functions are:

(i)   effective allocation of resources with attention to social and economic cost and to evolving budget structures that would better reflect development activities;

(ii) establishing budgetary policy and the budgetary management system as instruments of national economic management, communicating resource constraints to spending agencies, reducing gaps between planned and actual expenditures, and achieving better control of transfers;

---

[1]   FERD. https://ferd.gov.mm/about-us/.
[2]   Government of Myanmar. 2018. *Development Assistance Policy*. January 2018.
[3]   Ministry of Planning and Finance. https://www.mopfi.gov.mm/en/page/finance/%E1%80%9B%E1%80%9E%E1%80%AF%E1%80%B6%E1%80%B8%E1%80%99%E1%80%BE%E1%80%94%E1%80%BA%E1%80%81%E1%80%BC%E1%80%B1%E1%80%84%E1%80%BD%E1%80%B1%E1%80%85%E1%80%AC%E1%80%9B%E1%80%84%E1%80%BA%E1%80%B8%E1%80%A6%E1%80%B8%E1%80%85%E1%80%AE%E1%80%B8%E1%80%8C%E1%80%AC%E1%80%94/234].

(iii)   managing spending; and

(iv)   laying down financial and service rules and regulations for systematic management of spending and administration.

The department has several sections, of which the following are involved in foreign fund management.

Foreign Exchange Subdivision

Prepares foreign exchange budget, processes foreign exchange applications for agencies, and authorizes foreign exchange permits for the public sector in accordance with the annual budget.

State Administrative Organizations, Ministries and Departments Budget Division 1, Ministries and Departments Budget Division 2, State Economic Enterprises Budget Division, Compilation Subdivisions

Prepares and implements union-level annual budget, revised estimate budget, supplementary grant budget, and nonbudgetary receipts and payments.

Compilation Subdivision

Responsible for the formulation of the Union budget bill as well as Union supplementary budget bill and compiles data for ministries, departments, and SEEs for evaluation of the public sector budget.

Intergovernmental Fiscal Relation Division

Prepares and implements annual state and/or regional; budgets, supplementary grant budgets and nonbudgetary receipts and payments; controls and maintains staff records, salaries, wages, and expenses; and compiles the accounts of state and/or regional public sector budgets.

Service Regulation and Financial Regulation Division

Supervises financial regulations and administers rules of financial matters and service personnel; supervises gratuity, pension, and allowances for retirees; and publishes financial regulations guidance (most recently in 2017) for public sector entities on transaction control, consolidation, and reporting.

Treasury Department

This department was established in 2014 to manage and implement Union financial resources, including government bank accounts, cash flows, and cash assets. Its debt management section oversees external and domestic loan financing of the Union budget deficit and provides guidance. The Treasury Department takes a lead role in loan negotiation process and signing the financing agreement on behalf of the state.

Project Appraisal and Progress Reporting Department

The Project Appraisal and Progress Reporting Department (PAPRD) was established on 1 October 1972 and performed the functions of project appraisal. After 1988, PAPRD did not conduct the functions of project appraisal started the function of project monitoring since 2014. In 2019, PAPRD is required to appraise projects with government funding over MMK5 billion (about $3.6 million) and submit recommendations to the MOPF prior to approval.

Myanma Economic Bank

The Myanma Economic Bank (MEB) is a state-owned commercial public bank with seven head office departments, 14 state and/or regional offices, and 314 branches. All government institutions are allowed to carry out their transactions through MEB. The bank also maintains executing agencies' advance accounts for project loan agreements.

C. Central Bank of Myanmar

The Central Bank of Myanmar (CBM) was established under the Central Bank of Myanmar Law enacted on 2 July 1990, and became an independent and autonomous body by new Central Bank of Myanmar Law on 11 July 2013. The main aim of the Central Bank of Myanmar is to preserve and maintain domestic price stability. Its functions and powers as per the law are

(a) "formulating and implementing monetary policy;
(b) determining and implementing the exchange rate policy;
(c) advising to the government in respect of such exchange rate regime;
(d) maintaining and managing the international reserves of the state;
(e) acting as the sole issuer of, and managing, the domestic currency;
(f) overseeing the financial system and maintaining its stability;
(g) regulating and supervising financial institutions;
(h) overseeing the money market and foreign exchange market to ensure orderly operation in such markets;
(i) promoting and overseeing a safe, sound, and efficient payment system;
(j) acting as lender of last resort for banks;
(k) acting as a banker to the government by maintaining the accounts of the government;
(l) acting as financial advisor and fiscal agent to the government;
(m) acting as a banker for financial institutions, foreign governments, and international agencies;
(n) opening accounts with, and accepting deposits from, financial institutions;
(o) performing the transactions resulting from the participation of the state in international financial institutions in the banking, credit, and monetary sphere and undertaking the responsibilities in the name of the government dealing with the aforesaid organizations on behalf of the government; and
(p) carrying out such operations as may be consequential or incidental to the exercise of its powers and discharge of its duties under the Central Bank of Myanmar Law."[4]

[4] Government of Myanmar. 2013. *Central Bank of Myanmar Law. No. 16.* Unofficial Translation. http://www.asianlii.org/mm/legis/laws/cbomlhln162013505.pdf (accessed 4 January 2020).

D.   Office of the Auditor General

The Auditor General of the Union is appointed by the President as provisioned by section 242 of the Constitution of the Republic of the Union of Myanmar, 2008. Through the Auditor General of the Union Law No. 23 of 2010, he/she is mandated to audit the accounts of receipt and payment of the Union and report to the Union Parliament. This includes the accounts of all ministries, departments, agencies and state economic enterprises (SEEs). Region and/or state parliaments approve the appointment of respective auditors general who are responsible to the Auditor General of the Union, the Chief Minister of the relevant region/state, and the President of the Union through the Chief Minister of the relevant region and/or state. Detailed lists of responsibilities of the Auditor General of the Union and auditors general of regions and/or states are given in section VIII of this report.

E.   Asian Development Bank

Controller's Department

The Controller's Department, Loan Administration Division (CTLA) of ADB authorizes all loans, grants, and technical assistance disbursements. It is also responsible for maintaining accounting policy and systems, billing, collection, and accounting of loan service payments.

Myanmar Resident Mission

The Myanmar Resident Mission reviews all withdrawal applications received from the executing agency or project management unit (PMU) for direct payments and advance funds procedures, and forwards to CTLA for processing the disbursements.

III. Budgeting

A. Project Finance System

The Public Debt Management Law (2016) provides the legal mandate for the government to borrow money from local and foreign sources on behalf of the state, with the approval of the Union Parliament. This law authorizes the MOPF to borrow upon concluding loan agreements, issue government securities or enter into other credit agreements, and issue government guarantees. The law requires borrowing entities—the national government, region or state governments, development committees, and SEEs—to prioritize allocation of liabilities in their budgets. Note that Union Parliament approval is required for every loan obtained, while cabinet approval is adequate for grants.[5]

The MOPF is also permitted to issue loan guarantees on behalf of any person, entity, or projects with the approval of the Parliament. The Public Debt Management Law allows the MOPF to charge a fee on such guarantees and claim from the borrower: (i) all money disbursed by the government to fulfill the guarantee; (ii) all expenses incurred by the government in relation to the guarantee; and (iii) interest on all money disbursed by the government to fulfill the guarantee. Prior to the introduction of the law, the MOPF used to issue a letter of guarantee for loans.[6] Ministries, agencies, and SEEs seeking foreign financing assistance must have their proposals approved by the cabinet's economic committee for inclusion in the national budget.

The government introduced the Development Assistance Policy (DAP) in 2018, as a guideline for effective use of development assistance. As per this document, line ministries can identify initiatives requiring loan financing and initiate the process, while the MOPF takes the lead in negotiations and concluding loan agreements. The approval process for foreign-funded loans in Myanmar is captured in Figure 2 and detailed in the paragraphs that follow.

Initial discussions on proposed foreign-funded projects take place between development partners, relevant line ministries, and stakeholders of the MOPF. Ministries, agencies, and SEEs identify projects and submit their plans to the relevant line ministry for developing proposals in consultation with FERD, which then submits them to the Economic Committee. Proposals referred to the FERD in its capacity as DACU Secretariat, should include the following documents: (i) DACU and/or Economic Committee Project and/or Program Submission Form; (ii) Project and/or Program Design Document and Indicative

---

[5]   Based on meetings with Budget Department on 21 and 24 July 2017, and on process flow diagrams received.
[6]   Meeting with Union Budget Department on 24 July 2017.

Figure 2: Potential Myanmar Loan Approval Process

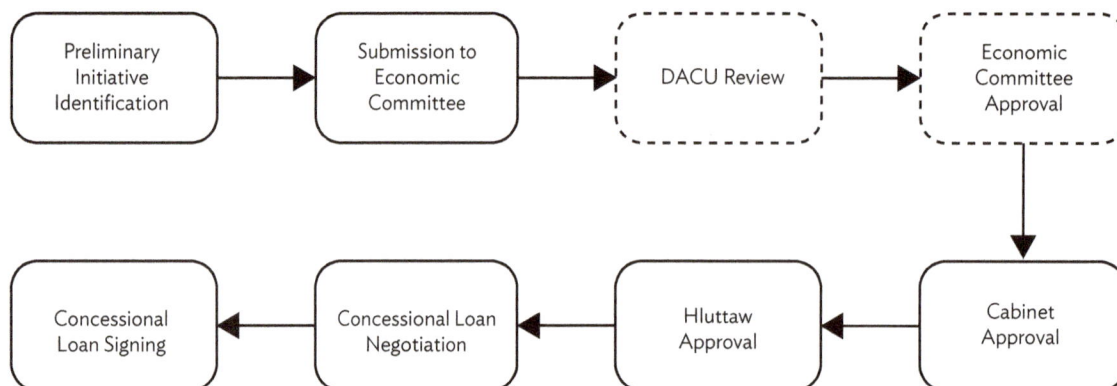

DACU = Development Assistance Coordination Unit.
Source: Government of Myanmar. 2018. *Development Assistance Policy*. January 2018.

Budget (if applicable); and (iii) Draft Concessional Loan Financing Agreement.[7] Guidelines and templates for preparation of proposals are provided in the DAP.

DACU, a high-level unit chaired by the state counselor, reviews foreign-funded development assistance proposals before they are submitted to the Economic Committee to ensure they aligned with national priorities.[8]

DACU advises the Economic Committee on foreign-funded proposals based on (i) alignment with national priorities, (ii) commercial effectiveness, and (iii) contribution toward sustainable development. PAPRD supports DACU in appraising projects with government contributions greater than MMK5 billion (~$3.6 million). PAPRD appraisals help to identify suitable financial options for proposed projects, such as government funds or public–private partnership arrangements.

The line ministry and/or executing agency submits loan proposals and required documents for a proposed project to the Economic Committee Secretariat and/or the MOPF. When the Economic Committee Secretariat receives a loan proposal, DACU assesses it against requirements and prepares the agenda for its submission to the Economic Committee. The Economic Committee assesses the proposal's consistency with national development priorities, and either approves, rejects, or requests revision or clarification.

If a proposal is approved, the line ministry and/or executing agency is informed by the Economic Committee Secretariat. The secretariat then prepares a concessional loan request package for signature and submission by the Union Minister for Planning and

---

[7]   Government of Myanmar. 2018. *Myanmar Sustainable Development Plan 2018–2030*. p. 39.
[8]   World Bank Group. 2017. *Myanmar Public Expenditure Review 2017: Fiscal Space for Economic Growth*. Yangon: World Bank. p. 30.

Figure 3: Potential Myanmar Grant Approval Process

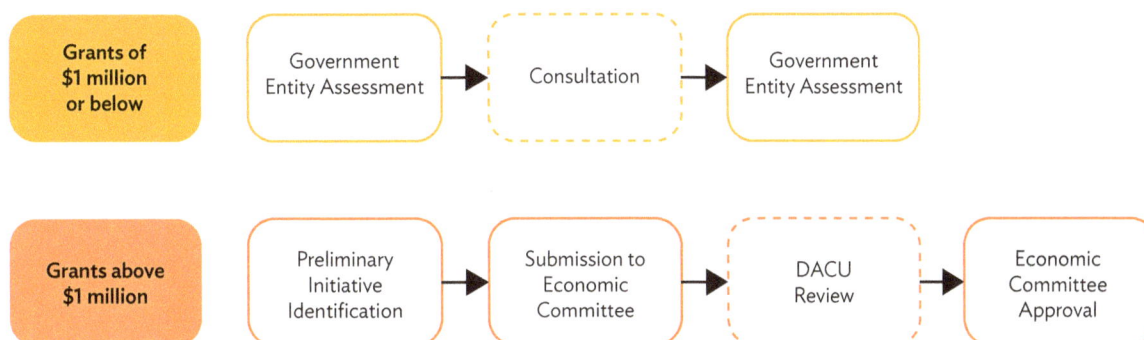

Grants of $1 million or below → Government Entity Assessment → Consultation → Government Entity Assessment

Grants above $1 million → Preliminary Initiative Identification → Submission to Economic Committee → DACU Review → Economic Committee Approval

DACU = Development Assistance Coordination Unit.
Source: Government of Myanmar. 2018. *Development Assistance Policy*. January 2018.

Finance to the cabinet. The cabinet considers the loan proposal and the views of the Economic Committee and either approves, rejects, or requests revision or clarification.

If approved, the Treasury Department prepares the required documentation in consultation with the line ministry and/or executing agency and development partner, and submits it to the President's office. The President requests the Union Parliament to review and debate the proposal. If approved, Parliament notifies the President's office, which in turn authorizes the Union Minister of Planning and Finance to officially request the concessional loan from the development partner. The DAP requires the development partner to register the concessional loan in the AIMS when it receives the MOPF request.

Loan negotiations commence thereafter, overseen by the MOPF. Representatives from the MOPF budget and treasury departments, FERD, Myanma Foreign Trade Bank, CBM, the Union Attorney General's Office, and the executing agency and/or line ministry form a concessional loan negotiation team. Once the concessional loan negotiation team accepts the terms and conditions of the Concessional Loan Financing Agreement, the Treasury Department submits the agreement to the Union Minister of Planning and Finance for signing.

For foreign-funded grants, the approval process is shorter as the Union Parliament is not involved. Grants worth $1.0 million (~MMK1.5 trillion) or below can be approved by the executing agency while grants above $1.0 million (~MMK1.5 trillion) can be approved by the Economic Committee. This threshold is defined in the DAP and will be reviewed on a regular basis by the government.[9] The grant approval process is captured in Figure 3 and detailed in the paragraphs that follow.

Grants worth $1 million or below do not require Economic Committee approval. The executing agency is responsible for consulting with relevant sector coordination groups to assess whether a proposal aligns with sector plans; and is consistent with, and complementary

---

[9]   Government of Myanmar. 2018. *Myanmar Sustainable Development Plan 2018–2030*. pp. 36–39.

to, other ongoing and planned initiatives. The grant is approved by the relevant Union Minister, Chief Minister, or similar authority. The executing agency confirms the approval to the development partner in writing, upon which the development partner is required to register the initiatives in AIMS. FERD is kept informed by submitting (i) the approval letter from the Union Minister, Chief Minister, or similar authority to the development partner; (ii) the approved Small Grant Summary Template (if applicable); (iii) the Project and/or Program Design Document and Indicative Budget (if applicable); and (iv) the Final Grant Agreement and/or Memorandum of Understanding or equivalent (if applicable). The DAP provides a standard Grant Agreement and/or Memorandum of Understanding template for this purpose. Executing agencies are required seek comment from the Office of the Auditor General (OAG) before approving the grant if nonstandard agreement templates are used or when proposed amendments are considered legally binding.[10]

Grants over $1 million follow the same approval process as loans, up to the point of Economic Committee assessment. Briefly, discussions are held between development partners, relevant executing agencies, and MOPF stakeholders to conceptualize a grant proposal. The executing agency ensures the proposed initiative aligns with sector plans and submits the DACU and/or Economic Committee Project and/or Program Submission Form, Project and/or Program Design Document and indicative budget (if applicable), and Draft Concessional Loan Financing Agreement, as defined in the DAP. Prior to submission to the Economic Committee, DACU evaluates whether a proposal aligns with national priorities.

The Economic Committee assesses the proposal's consistency with national development priorities, and either approves, rejects, or requests revision or clarification. If approved, the line ministry and/or executing agency is informed and can sign the grant. The executing agency informs the relevant development partner to register the initiative in the AIMS.

A recent World Bank report notes that project selection is ad hoc, that projects are not systematically appraised before budget creation, and that while Myanmar has made progress by developing appraisal guidelines, critical gaps remain in regulation and appraisal capacity.[11] It suggests that the newly introduced DACU offers a good opportunity to set the strategic framework for overseas development assistance by: (i) clarifying roles and responsibilities of different agencies in reviewing and approving overseas development assistance proposals; (ii) creating fiscal space for public services and infrastructure; and (iii) strengthening principles of aid management, including efforts to increasingly use and strengthen government systems.

The report also cites a 2016 MOPF review (supported by the World Bank) of Myanmar's public investment management systems and processes across eight standard good practice functions. It notes that projects are not systematically and comprehensively appraised because while appraisal was reinstated in 2012, in practice, this function is curtailed due to the lack of a formal legal mandate, limited and inadequate safeguards, and limited capacity.

The government recently published the Myanmar Sustainable Development Plan, 2018–2030 as a holistic development framework offering coherence to existing strategic

---

[10]   Government of Myanmar. 2018. *Myanmar Sustainable Development Plan 2018–2030*. p. 37.
[11]   Footnote 8.

documents, and ensuring they are executed in ways consistent with macro-level national development priorities. The plan comprises 3 pillars, 5 goals, 28 strategies, and 251 action plans that are expected to provide an overall framework for coordination and cooperation across all agencies toward sustainable development.[12]

B.   The Union Fund

Based on the 2008 Constitution, in 2011, Myanmar replaced its single state public fund with a Union Fund for the union-level ministries and agencies, and region and/or state funds for region- and/or state-level organizations.

The Union government is required to collect all taxes and revenues and deposit them in the Union Fund, excluding those listed in Schedule Five of the Constitution, which are collected by regions and/or states. The Minister of Planning and Finance authorizes spending agencies to use the funds allocated to them under the budget law from the Union Fund.

Any transfers to regions and/or states from the Union Fund should be recommended by the Finance Commission and included in the budget law. The Finance Commission is a committee formed and chaired by the President based on the Constitution (Section 229a) and the Union Government Law (Section 11a). Members comprise Vice-Presidents, the Attorney General, the Auditor General, the Chairperson of Nay Pyi Taw Council, chief ministers, and the Minister of Finance as a secretary. The role of the Finance Commission is to (i) submit its recommendations for the Union budget and transfers from the Union budget; (ii) advise the Parliament on financial matters as applicable; and (iii) carry out any other activities as assigned by the Parliament.

The Union government finances the budget deficits and special matters of the regions and/or states. The government used to finance region-level SEE budget deficits by providing loans with a 4% interest rate, but this practice was abandoned in fiscal year (FY) 2016. All budget deficits at state and/or region level are now financed by the Union via grant transfers considering six indicators during the budget preparing stage: (i) total population; (ii) poverty index; (iii) area; (iv) urban population as percentage of total state population; (v) per capita tax collection; and (vi) per capita gross domestic product.[13]

Financing of special matters of states and/or regions from the Union Fund follow the government's annual policy guidelines. Examples of funds at the state and/or region level financed by the Union are the Regional Development and Poverty Alleviation Fund (from FY2013 to FY2016), the Regional Development Fund (since FY2014–FY2015 RE), the Township Development and Management Fund (from FY2016), the One-Stop Service Office for District and/or Township (FY2016), the Rental Housing Project (FY2016), and the Farmland Development Fund (FY2016).[14]

---

[12]   Government of Myanmar. 2018. *Myanmar Sustainable Development Plan 2018–2030*.
[13]   SS Oo. 2016. *Fiscal Management Reform in Myanmar (Lessons Drawn from Japanese Experiences)*. Paper by Visiting Scholar from the Policy Research Institute, Ministry of Finance, Japan.
[14]   Footnote 13.

C.   Budget Recording and Reporting

The Budget Department of the MOPF is tasked with ensuring effective resource allocation and monitoring budget implementation. Following Myanmar's Medium-Term Fiscal Framework, line ministries are required to handle public funds allocated to them in the budget law through MEB and submit monthly and quarterly reports to the MOPF. Additionally, the National Planning and Finance Committee and the Public Account Committee (PAC) were formed to provide budgetary oversight. The National Planning and Finance Committee reviews the national development plan and legislative matters while the PAC reviews the budget bill and audit reports.

D.   Budget Process

The legal framework for budget preparation originates from the Constitution of the Republic of the Myanmar 2008, section 103. The President or his assigned representative is required to submit the budget bill to Parliament and obtain approval to use Union Funds.

Myamnar's Sustainable Development Plan, 2018–2030, serves as the overall development framework for the country. Drawing up the national plan, annual plan, and 5-year medium-term plan is the responsibility of the MOPF. This was formerly done by the Ministry of National Planning and Economic Development, which was merged with the Ministry of Finance in 2016 to form the MOPF. The MOPF also prepares the medium-term fiscal framework based on the national plan. Agencies are required to submit their budget proposals for capital expenditure in line with the annual plan.[15]

The budget process in Myanmar is decentralized. Union administrative organizations and line ministries submit their estimates to the MOPF Budget Department. While regions and/or states are empowered with their own parliament and affairs, any transfers to these regions and/or states from the Union have to be recommended by the Finance Commission. State/region-level institutions submit their budget estimates to region and/or state budget offices, who then submit them to the MOPF Budget Department. SEE budgets are included as part of the budget of the relevant line ministry under which they operate. Budgets are scrutinized by the two Vice-Presidents (union-level and region-and/or state-level) and submitted to the Parliament by the President. The approved budget bill is promulgated as the Union Budget Law in September. The process for requesting supplementary allocations during the fiscal year is similar and results in the annual Supplementary Budget Law in May.

The Myanmar government expenditure comprises of current, capital, and financial expenditures. The current expenditure accounts for the largest portion, with 75% of the total expenditure in the 2017–2018 budget estimates, whereas capital expenditure and financial expenditure accounted for 22% and 3% respectively.[16]

---

[15]   Footnote 13.
[16]   Government of Myanmar. 2017. *Citizen's Budget 2017–2018 Fiscal Year Budget Information.* Ministry of Planning and Finance.

E.   Central Budget

Until 2017, annual budgets were arranged for the fiscal year, which started 1 April and ended 31 March the following year. The budget formulation process started in September for the next fiscal year. Effective from October 2018, the government has declared that the fiscal year will run 1 October–30 September.

A budget letter, including ceilings, is issued to the spending agencies for the preparation of the budget estimates. Estimates submitted by the agencies are then examined by the MOPF Budget Department (recurrent expenditures) or by the Construction Works Committee, Equipment Control Committee, and the MOPF Planning Department (capital expenditures). Discussions and negotiations are then held with the agencies.

Foreign-funded project expenditures are included in line ministry budgets at the union-level only if the loan or grant agreements have been approved by the Parliament.

Under the 2008 Constitution, the budgets of Union ministries and union-level organizations must be vetted by a Vice-President assigned by the President, and then submitted to the Finance Commission. If any changes are made, the MOPF Budget Department informs the concerned agencies. The revised budget is then submitted to the Union cabinet by the Finance Commission as the Recommendation Budget Bill.

The President submits the Union Budget Bill to Parliament. Once approved, the bill is signed by the President and promulgated as the Union Budget Law. Appendixes 1 and 2 depict the timeline for preparing the budget estimates of the Union.

Local Budget

The Budget Department of the Union MOPF calculates appropriation of funds for regions and/or states based on the medium-term financial framework (MTFF) and other financial data indicators and issues information to the respective region or state governments through the Union government. The region- and/or state-level departments and organizations prepare their budget statements with the approval of heads of respective head offices or departments, and submit to the respective region and/or state Budget Department. The region and/or state Budget Department prepares the budget statement of respective regions and/or states based on appropriation regarding grants for the budget deficits of regions and/or states from the Union Fund and submits the statements to the respective region and/or state governments.

The region and/or state government scrutinizes the budget statement submitted by the respective Budget Department and submits to the respective region and/or state parliament (or hluttaw) for approval. The region and/or state Budget Departments submit their budget statements that are approved by the respective hluttaw to the Budget Department of the Union MOPF within the specified date.

The Budget Department of the Union MOPF compiles budget statements submitted by regions and/or states Budget Department, and submits to the Union Minister of Planning and Finance for submission to the Vice-President to obtain approval, and submit thereafter to the Financial Commission and Union government. Once the Union Budget Law is enacted, the Union Government Office informs the region and/or state governments about grants from the Union Fund for them.

The Budget Departments of regions and/or states check the grants allocated from the Union Fund by the Union Government Office with the budget statements permitted by the region and/or state hluttaw and amend as necessary. The region and/or state budget bill under the budget statements are then drafted and submitted to the region and/or state governments for approval by the region and/or state hluttaw. Once approved, the Chief Minister of the region and/or state signs their respective bill and promulgates it as their region and/or state budget law.[17] Appendix 3 shows the timeline for preparing the budget estimates of regions and/or states.

F.   Budgetary Channel

Relationship between Disbursement and Budget Plan

Budget allocations at ministry and department levels are based on estimates they provide that are approved by Parliament. Though these estimates go into economic classification (minor and subheadings), such detail is not necessary for Parliament approval and is more relevant for budget holders submitting monitoring reports to the Budget Department.[18]

The annual budget law also calls for aggregate information on capital spending (including loans financed), external borrowing, and grant funding by ministries. Spending agencies are required to provide estimates of their quarterly cash needs for recurrent expenditures a quarter in advance. These are provided to MEB and become their quarterly limits, which must not be exceeded. A limit will be removed from the year as a whole if not used within the quarter. Spending agencies can manage this risk by avoiding over estimation and seeking increases in limits later in the quarters when necessary.[19]

Through the DAP, the government has put in place a monitoring and evaluation framework, expected to strengthen the effectiveness, transparency, and accountability of development assistance.[20]

There is room for improvement in overall budget execution in Myanmar. Better planning to minimize use of supplementary budgets, and timely approval of supplementary budgets when used, could help address delays in implementation. So could delegation of duties with clear guidelines and government-wide operating procedures on critical aspects of financial management. However, the lack of adequate numbers of sufficiently trained financial management staff will continue to pose a challenge in implementation.[21]

---

[17]   Government of Myanmar. 2008. *The Constitution of the Republic of the Myanmar 2008.* (Section 195).

[18]   World Bank. 2013. *Republic of the Union of Myanmar - Public financial management performance report (Vol. 2).* Washington, DC: World Bank. p. 66.

[19]   Footnote 18, pp. 44, 56, and 66.

[20]   Government of Myanmar. 2018. *Myanmar Sustainable Development Plan 2018–2030.* p. 52.

[21]   Footnote 8, p. 19.

Accounting for Foreign Funds

Foreign funds are accounted for in the government's accounting system, and spending units should be able to budget and report on aid transferred in cash. It is noted, however, that for in-kind aid, the government depends on the donor for information on budget estimates and spending. Donor cash disbursements reports are also an important tool for reconciliation with government project accounts.

As in other countries, obtaining reliable information on foreign aid commitments and disbursements is a challenge. In this regard, the country is seeking to strengthen its AIMS through two initiatives: (i) the Myanmar Information Management Unit 3W (Who does What, Where) database, with detailed project and/or village-level information—though not spending information; and (ii) the Mohinga database, which records project commitments and disbursements, directly following the standards set by the International Aid Transparency Initiative, at the sector, donor, or project level.[22]

G. Internal Controls

Expenditure Controls

Expenditure control happens at different levels within government spending agencies. The Minister of Planning and Finance has the overall responsibility for supervision of public finance administration in the country. Ministry directorates control allotment of funds for officers and positions are identified at each level with responsibility for budget execution and financial management. Within an organization, internal checks including segregation of duties facilitate expenditure control. Expenditures are also subjected to audit by the Auditor General and parliamentary review through the PAC.

Financial regulations and instructions, provided through the *Oo Sa* (guidance document on the accounting system and fiscal reporting in Myanmar) and *Tha Sa* (guidance document on procedural rules for maintenance of accounts and formats for reporting), lay down guidance for directorates and drawing officers under their control, primarily targeting avoidance of overspending of budget allocations. However, there is no guarantee that processes followed by spending bodies meet minimum procedures and controls due to a lack of centrally defined standards for some critical spending dimensions.[23]

Internal Audit

The 2013 World Bank report identified weak internal control and the lack of an internal audit function in many spending bodies.[24] The absence of internal auditing in line ministries provides inadequate assurance to senior management with regard to accuracy and control of systems and procedures. The report notes that although internal audit units are required in all large-scale public bodies, in practice, they are not available. SEEs under ministries have internal audit units with varying effectiveness while some ministries have inspection units

---

[22] Footnote 8, p. 30.
[23] Footnote 18, p. 57.
[24] Footnote 18, pp. 8–10.

that conduct prepayment checks, but cannot be considered internal audits.[25] Our study also indicates that internal auditing is an area that requires strengthening.

Reporting and Monitoring

PMUs report to their parent ministries or agencies. Moreover, PMUs have collective reporting responsibilities toward the government and the donors, including:

(i)   submitting expenditure statements to the relevant ministry on a monthly basis and to the Treasury Department on a weekly and monthly basis;

(ii) providing spending information to the relevant ministry on a quarterly basis (who then should report donor-related spending estimates to FERD on a quarterly basis);

(iii) preparing and submitting monthly and fiscal year-end accounts to the relevant ministry and/or executing agency; and preparing and submitting annual financial statements to external auditors (auditors general) and forwarding the audited statements to the donor.

All projects are subject to monitoring by PAPRD, based on an annual rolling project monitoring plan approved by the Minister of Planning and Finance. Teams are deployed to the field for monitoring according to the plan, where project status, including completion rate and level of financial spending, are checked and evidence gathered. Reports submitted by field officers with status, reasons for delays, constraints faced, and recommendations to overcome constraints are reviewed by PAPRD and submitted to the relevant line ministries. Quarterly reports on project monitoring are shared with relevant line ministries, the Minister's Office of the MOPF, Planning Department, Budget Department, OAG, and President's office. The line ministries are required to respond to issues highlighted in the report.

---

[25]   Footnote 18, pp. 77 and 79.

IV. Onlending Arrangements

Through the Public Debt Management Law (2016), the government (with the approval of the Union Parliament) is allowed to borrow from local and foreign sources. Chapter II of the law stipulates valid reasons for borrowing[26] and authorizes the Minister of Planning and Finance to borrow or guarantee borrowing by other organizations on behalf of the government.[27] The policies and guidelines for lending and onlending, and issuance of debt guarantees are stipulated in this document along with other debt management-related matters and all borrowings should be approved by the Parliament. The law also mandates the MOPF to prepare a medium-term debt management strategy annually.

Onlent or subgranted foreign loans obtained by the government are administered through subsidiary loan agreements and are signed by the Director General of the Treasury Department of MOPF. Key decisions on onlending or subgranting, such as currency to be used, are made during the program and/or project negotiation stage with the development partner.

Union-level organizations. Foreign funds for all ministries and agencies under the Union government are always allocated through the Union budget under the respective budget headings, and are approved by Parliament. These entities are entitled to withdraw funds from the Union Fund against their budget allocations. Although the central government borrows in foreign currency, the allocations to ministries and agencies are made in local currency.

Region- and/or state-level organizations. The MOPF borrows and onlends in the same currency as the main loan to the regions and/or states through a subsidiary agreement. Provisions for these funds are made in the Union budget under the MOPF budget head and are also included in the respective region and/or state budgets. The Public Debt Management Law (2016) also allows regions and/or states to borrow on their own, with the approval of the Union government and Union Parliament.[28]

SEEs. Foreign borrowing for SEEs is onlent through a subsidiary agreement and is reflected in the Union budget. SEE budgets are included in the budgets of their respective line ministries.

---

[26] Government of Myanmar. 2016. *Myanmar Public Debt Management Law, 2016.* (Chapter II, section 3).
[27] Footnote 26, (Chapter II, section 5).
[28] Footnote 26, (Chapter II, section 20).

V. Foreign Exchange and Interest Rate Risks

Foreign exchange and interest rate risks for subgrants to line ministries are borne by the Union and the amounts are included in the budgets of the respective line ministries.

Interest rate risks of onlent funds to the states and/or regions are passed on to the sub-borrower, as well as responsibility for repayment of the loan, as specified in the subsidiary loan agreement. The sub-borrower must factor in yearly foreign currency amounts in their repayment budgets. The exchange rate considered for the conversion is fixed at the date of approval and any exchange gain or loss incurred during the year is borne by the government. Agencies can request additional foreign currency, which will be submitted to the Budget Department and approved by the Minister of Planning and Finance.

VI. Funds Flow Arrangements

Funds flow arrangements are specified in the respective project administration manual as agreed on between the government and ADB. As part of the prerequisites for withdrawals from loan and/or grant accounts, the MOPF submits to ADB evidence of authority of the persons who will be signing the withdrawal applications.

Of the four categories of ADB funds flow arrangements, in Myanmar, direct payment and advance fund procedures are common, while reimbursement and commitment procedures have not been used for ADB projects to date.[29] Direct payment and advance fund procedures are discussed below, detailing the funds flow, recording in government accounts, transfer of funds between government agencies, and documents required under each arrangement.[30] Reimbursement and commitment procedures are not discussed since the government has never used these methods. Guidelines in the *ADB Loan Disbursement Handbook* should be followed if the situation changes.

A. Direct Payment Procedure

The funds flow under this procedure is solely between ADB and the contractor, consultant, or supplier. The PMU requests ADB to transfer funds for the expenses incurred directly to the contractor, consultant, or supplier by withdrawal from the loan and/or grant account.

Funds Flow

The steps involved in the direct payment procedure are described below and illustrated in Figure 5, while required documentation is shown in Table 1:

(i) The PMU receives expense invoices from the contractor or supplier. In the event a project consultant is appointed by the PMU, he or she will receive the invoices and issue an interim payment certificate to the PMU after verification.

(ii) The PMU verifies the details and submits a withdrawal application (signed by the authorized person) and supporting documents to Myanmar Resident Mission. A copy is sent to the executing agency and the MOPF Treasury Department for reference purposes.

---

[29] Study period was from April to July 2017.
[30] In case of conflict between ADB's procedures described in this report and the procedures in ADB's guidelines (Loan Disbursement Handbook, 2017, or as amended from time to time), the procedures in ADB's guidelines will prevail.

Figure 4: Direct Payment Procedure

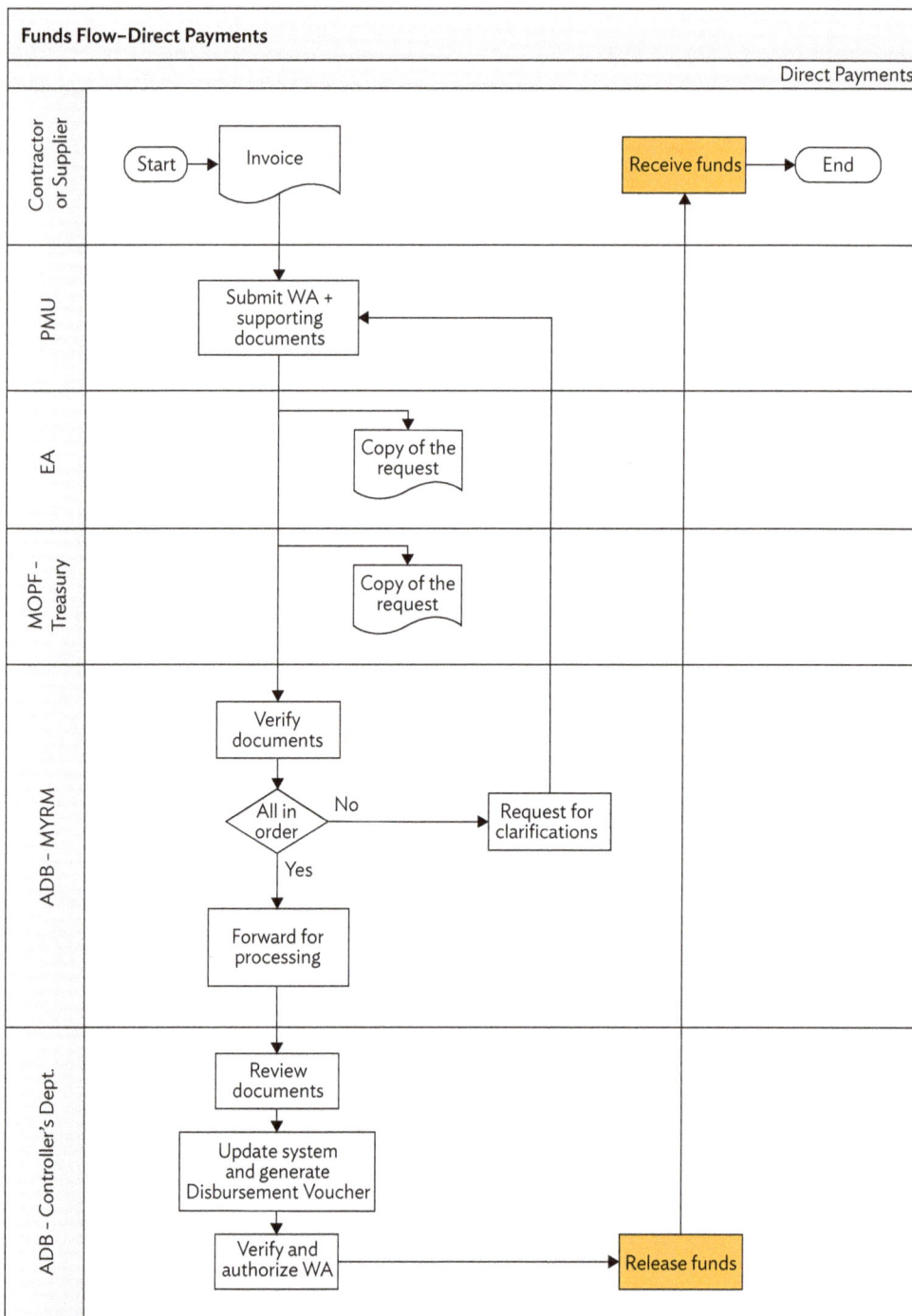

ADB = Asian Development Bank, EA = executing agency, MOPF = Ministry of Planning and Finance, MYRM = Myanmar Resident Mission, PMU = project management unit, WA = withdrawal application.

Note: Flowchart based on discussions with government stakeholders.

Source: Asian Development Bank.

(iii)   After receiving the withdrawal application (WA) with the supporting documents from Myanmar Resident Mission, CTLA reviews the received documents, inputs its details into the ADB internal processing system with generating the disbursement voucher if the withdrawal application is in order.
(iv)   CTLA verifies and authorizes the withdrawal application.
(v)   Upon receipt of CTLA's authorization, the ADB Treasury Department remits funds directly to the contractor or supplier's account.

Recording in the government accounts

Accounts are maintained in Microsoft Excel. The PMU submits to the MOPF Treasury Department a weekly statement, and a monthly statement, a copy of which goes to the executing agency for preparation of its monthly financial statements.

Documentary and approval requirements

The withdrawal application must be signed by the authorized signatories for the project.

Table 1: Documents Required for Fund Disbursement under Direct Payment Procedure

Payment for	Payment Type	Required Supporting Documents
Goods	One-time or installment payment	Supplier's invoice, or purchase order (indicating date, amount, and bank account details)
Services	Advance payment	Consultant's or service provider's invoice (indicating amount of advance payment and bank account details)
	Progress payment	Consultant's or service provider's invoice (indicating date, amount, and bank account details)
Civil works	Advance payment	Contractor's invoice (indicating date, amount, and bank account details)
	Progress payment	Contractor's invoice and interim payment certificate or summary of work progress (indicating period covered, amount, and bank account details)
	Release of retention money	Contractor's invoice (indicating date, amount, and bank account details) and unconditional bank guarantee (if required under section 4.27 of *ADB Loan Disbursement Handbook*)
Others		Depending on project specific requirements provided in the Project Administration Manual (PAM), the contract, or other legal documents

Source: Asian Development Bank. 2017. *Loan Disbursement Handbook*. Manila: Asian Development Bank.

B.   Advance Fund Procedure

An advance account (previously called the imprest account) in foreign currency is maintained at MEB by the executing agency following each loan or grant agreement.

The executing agency opens a Ministry and Department Account (known as an MD account) at MEB for funds converted from foreign to local currency. With the approval of the MOPF, PMUs open an "Other Account" (known as an OA account) into which it receives fund transfers from the MD account of the executing agency.

Under the advance fund procedure, ADB remits an advance to the advance account to exclusively finance ADB's share of eligible project expenditures of the respective project, based on the request from the government. The details of this procedure are in the project administration manual.

Funds Flow

The steps involved in the advance fund procedure are described below and illustrated in Figure 6, while required documentation is shown in Table 2:

Receipt of advance from ADB:

(i)   The PMU forecasts expenditures for the next 6 months and submits them to the executing agency for approval.

(ii)   Upon approval, the PMU submits a withdrawal application and supporting documents to Myanmar Resident Mission. A copy is sent to the executing agency and the MOPF Treasury Department for reference purposes.

(iii) After receiving the WA with supporting documents from Myanmar Resident Mission, CTLA reviews the received documents, and if the WA is in order, puts its details into ADB's internal processing system with generating the disbursement voucher.

(iv)   CTLA verifies and authorizes the withdrawal application.

(v)   Upon receipt of CTLA's authorization, the ADB Treasury Department remits funds to the advance account at MEB.

Fund transfer to subaccount:

(i)   The PMU submits a Proposal Letter to the executing agency for withdrawal of funds from the advance account.

(ii)   The executing agency approves the request and advises MEB for fund transfer.

(iii) MEB transfers the funds to the PMU's subaccount. The executing agency is informed of the remittances through the monthly bank statements.

Payments to the contractor or supplier

(i)   The contractor or supplier submits the invoice to the PMU.

(ii)   After checking the invoice details, the PMU makes the payment from its subaccount.

(iii) The PMU submits monthly expense statements to the MOPF Treasury Department.

Liquidation and/or replenishments from ADB

(i)   The PMU submits a withdrawal application and supporting documents to Myanmar Resident Mission. A copy is sent to the executing agency and the MOPF Treasury Department for reference purposes.

(ii) After receiving the WA with the supporting documents from Myanmar Resident Mission, CTLA reviews and verifies the received documents, and, if the withdrawal application is in order, puts its details into the ADB internal processing system, generating the disbursement voucher.

(iii) CTLA verifies and authorizes the withdrawal application.

(iv) Upon receipt of CTLA's authorization, the ADB Treasury Department remits funds to the advance account at MEB.

Figure 5: Advance Fund Procedure

Funds Flow–Imprest Funds

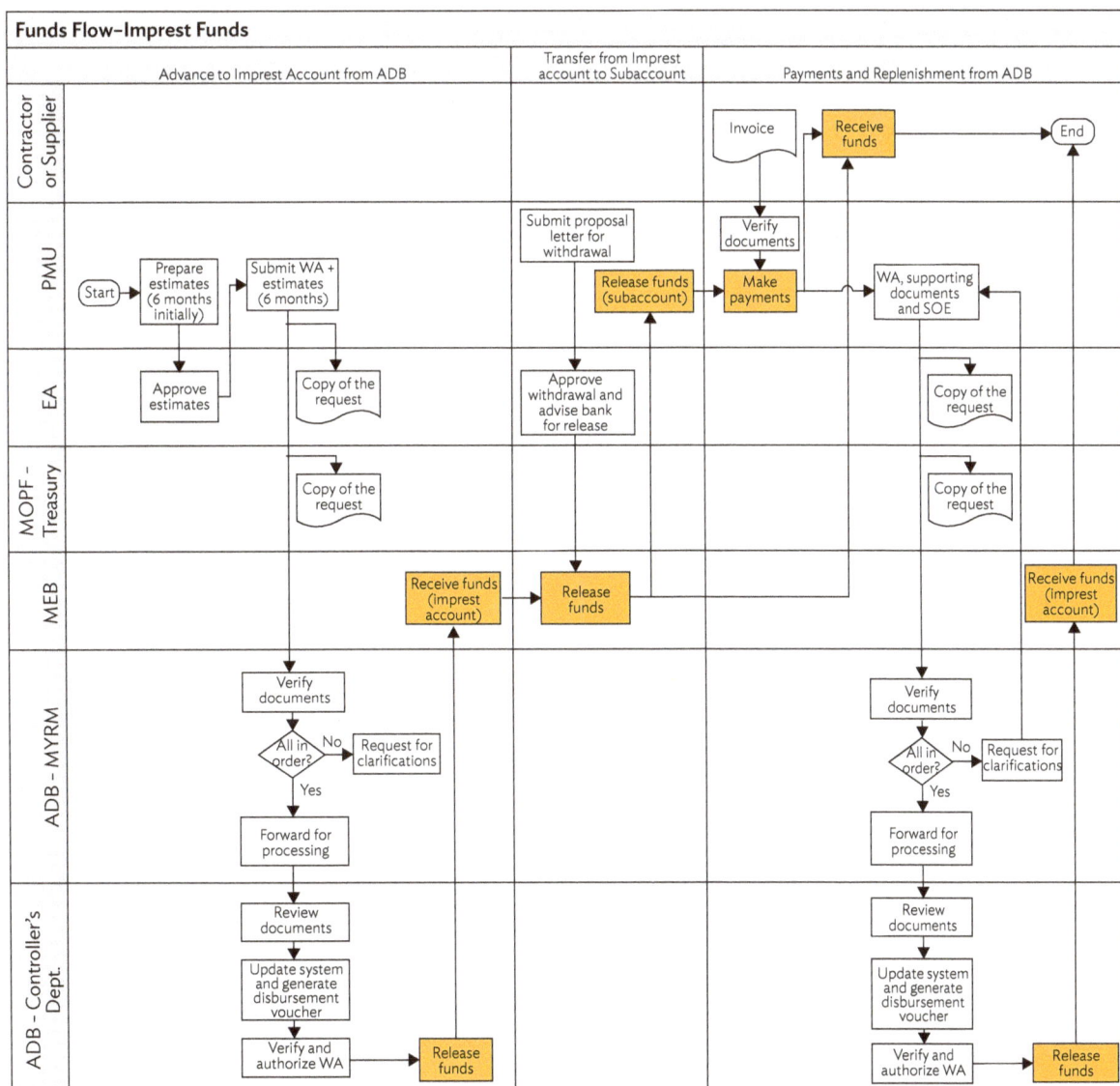

ADB = Asian Development Bank, EA = executing agency, MEB = Myanma Economic Bank, MOPF = Ministry of Planning and Finance, MYRM = Myanmar Resident Mission, PMU = project management unit, WA = withdrawal application.
Note: Flowchart based on discussions with government stakeholders.
Source: Asian Development Bank.

Recording in the government accounts

Accounts are maintained in Microsoft Excel. The PMU submits to the MOPF Treasury Department a weekly statement, and a monthly statement, a copy of which goes to the executing agency for preparation of its monthly financial statements.

Documentary and approval requirements

The withdrawal application must be signed by the authorized signatories for the project.

Table 2: Documents Required for Fund Disbursement under Advance Fund Procedure

Item	Required Supporting Documents
Initial advance and additional advance	Estimate of expenditure (Appendix 8A of *ADB Loan Disbursement Handbook*) to support the amount of the initial advance and the additional advance (see also sections 8.12 and 8.19 of *ADB Loan Disbursement Handbook*).
Liquidation and replenishment, or liquidation only	Advance account reconciliation statement (Appendix 8B of *ADB Loan Disbursement Handbook*) Ending balance per the corresponding bank statement Summary or SOE sheet (Appendix 7B or 7D of *ADB Loan Disbursement Handbook*) and supporting documents (see section 7.6 of *ADB Loan Disbursement Handbook*), if SOE procedure is not used. In addition, if FAW certificate procedure is used, and the amounts requested to be withdrawn are paid from the advance fund, the certificates for FAW (Appendix 7E of *ADB Loan Disbursement Handbook*) need to be attached to the withdrawal application.

FAW = force account for works.
Source: Asian Development Bank. 2017. *Loan Disbursement Handbook*. Manila: Asian Development Bank.

VII. Accounting and Reporting

A. Accounting Standards

As per the Myanmar Accountancy Council Law (2015), the Myanmar Accountancy Council (MAC) is the regulatory body of the country, and is chaired by the Union Auditor General. Its duties and powers, among others, include advising on requirements for accountancy, and accounting of government departments and business entities. With regard to accounting standards, the Myanmar Institute of Certified Public Accountants is a national accountancy body.

B. Public and Private Companies

As per the Myanmar Companies Act, corporations must prepare their financial statements in accordance with Myanmar Accounting Standards. The Securities and Exchange Rules and Regulations also require that public companies prepare their accounts based on Myanmar Financial Reporting Standards (MFRS).

In 2003 and 2004, MAC issued Myanmar Accounting Standards 1 to 30, which were based on international accounting standards existing at that time. Because they lacked detailed guidance, MAC replaced them in 2011 with 29 new standards and 8 new MFRSs identical to the 2010 International Financial Reporting Standards. Myanmar has also adopted the International Financial Reporting Standards for small and medium-sized enterprises (SMEs) as the MFRS for SMEs.[31] Nevertheless, there remains a significant gap between the requirements of the accounting standards and the actual practice across organizations. The World Bank Report on Observance of Standards and Codes (ROSC) notes that MAC is in discussions with the International Financial Reporting Standards Foundation on the adoption of the international standards, with notification to be published in the government gazette.[32]

MFRS is required for all domestic and foreign companies registered in Myanmar, including SMEs. SMEs are permitted to use the MFRS for SMEs or the general MFRS.

---

[31] PwC. 2014. *Myanmar Business Guide: Accounting and Auditing Regulations in Myanmar.* p. 22.
[32] World Bank. 2017. *Myanmar - Report on Observance of Standards and Codes (ROSC): accounting and auditing module* (English). Washington, DC: World Bank Group. p. 28.

C.   State-Owned Economic Enterprises

The State-Owned Economic Enterprises Act (1989) sets the regulatory framework for governance of SEEs, but allows the parent line ministry to determine the duties, powers, governance, and financial arrangements of an SEE.[33]

SEEs in Myanmar follow generally accepted accounting principles (GAAP), applying a double-entry accounting system with some accrual entries incorporated into financial statements.[34] These accounting standards do not fully comply with international best practices.[35]

D.   Government Sector Units

Outside of SEEs, other government sector units follow GAAP using a double-entry accounting system. It is noted that the MOPF and the OAG intend to transition the accounting system to align with International Public Sector Accounting Standards (IPSAS).

E.   Financial Regulations

Myanmar revised its previously outdated (revised in 1986) financial regulations in 2017. The regulations, along with instructions given through the guidance documents *Hta Sa*, *Oo Sa*, and *Sa Ya*, provide guidance to the public sector entities on transaction control, consolidation, and reporting. The guidance in the *Hta Sa*, *Oo Sa*, and *Sa Ya* is based on the accounting system introduced in 1972. The *Hta Sa* provides procedural rules for maintenance of accounts and formats for reporting to be followed by drawing officers at primary accounting units in all departments of government.[36] The *Oo Sa* provides guidance to directorates on consolidating accounts received from primary accounting units and compiling monthly accounts for submission to the Budget Department. These accounts are consolidated by the Treasury Department based on the guidance in the *Sa Ya*.

It is noted that the State-Owned Economic Enterprises Act (1989) under which SEEs are established does not contain specific provisions related to statutory financial reporting or auditing. Hence, statutory requirements of financial reporting and auditing of SEEs is determined by the type of enterprise. SEEs follow the Financial Management Rules and Regulations of Myanmar issued by the MOPF.[37]

The *Oo Sa* requires that main accounts of the government be maintained in accordance with the principles of government accounting. Receipts and expenditure of commercial undertakings must also be accounted under the appropriate major and minor headings as ordinary receipts and expenditure of the government. This facilitates the preparation of monthly income and expenditure statements from the general ledger maintained at all government undertakings.

---

[33]   Footnote 8, p. 70.
[34]   It is noted that there are no accounting standards as such.
[35]   Footnote 32, p. 18.
[36]   Except accounting of expenditure on works of the forest department and irrigation department.
[37]   Footnote 32, p. 17.

However, to visualize the financial details of commercial undertakings, separate books are maintained in accordance with commercial principles. The *Oo Sa* requires any commercial undertaking of the government to strictly observe essential formalities of commercial accounts, if the government so desires. These are pro forma accounts and are maintained outside of the government's regular accounts.

F.   Application of Accounting Standards and Regulations

Application of accounting standards and regulations by government entities varies by type of entity. As indicated previously, the government sector follows GAAP; financial reporting and auditing of government entities, including unincorporated SEEs, are based on the Financial Management Rules and Regulations; and incorporated SEEs follow the Companies Act or Special Companies Act.

The World Bank Public Finance Management Performance Report 2013 noted that spending agencies followed a mix of rules, with finance departments appearing to play a key role in determining the mix adopted, adoption varying from ministry to ministry, and interpretation of rules left open to financial management officials.[38] An ADB working paper in 2015, also identified that lack of clear operating guidelines for critical spending dimensions, such as procurement and payroll management, lead to spending agencies developing their own detailed procedures and systems on matters that should be subject to government-wide standards.[39] Discussions during our field mission also confirmed that this is still an issue.

G.   Accounting System

Basis of Accounting

As per the accounting system and fiscal reporting of Myanmar (*Oo Sa*), government accounts are maintained on a cash basis and follow the national budget headings. Transactions in government accounts, except for book adjustments authorized by general or special orders of the government, will be representative of actual cash receipts and disbursements.

Accounting Documents

The drawing officers of primary accounting units are required to maintain the following documents of accounts:

(i)   Form *Hta Sa*-5 Cash Book
(ii)   Form *Hta Sa*-6 Cash Balance Statement

---

[38]   Footnote 18, p. 9.
[39]   Z. Oo et al. 2015. *Fiscal Management in Myanmar. ADB Economics Working Paper Series* No. 434. Manila: Asian Development Bank.

(iii)   Form *Hta Sa*-7 Bank Receipts Book
(iv)   Form *Hta Sa*-8 Bank Payments Book
(v)   Form *Hta Sa*-9 Register for Cash by Detailed Headings
(vi)   Form *Hta Sa*-10 Monthly Cash Statement
(vii) Form *Hta Sa*-11 Monthly Bank Reconciliation Statement
(viii) Form *Hta Sa*-12 Plus and Minus Account Table for Debt and Deposit Account
(ix)   Form *Hta Sa*-13 Petty Cash Book

The *Hta Sa* provides instructions and formats for the preparation of these documents.

Chart of Accounts

Projects are required to maintain accounts meeting the reporting requirements of the government and the donor. Government accounts are maintained in accordance with budget headings while transactions are recorded under an elaborate classification system to instill uniformity. Projects are required to follow the same government classification system in their reporting to the directorate.

Accounting Method

Government accounts are maintained on a cash basis and are kept in accordance with government accounting principles. The majority of the government accounts are based on a single-entry system while double-entry is used only for a set of technical accounts. ADB-funded projects are required to maintain separate accounts and records in accordance with ADB principles.

Computerized Accounting System and Level of Automation

The government accounting system is paper-based and lacks a centralized system that gives a consolidated picture of Myanmar's financial position. Previous studies note that the manual ledger system in use is nevertheless largely up-to-date and reasonably accurate.[40] Computerization of the system was identified as a target in the PFM System Reformation Strategy 2013–2025. The strategy lays out the development of a sophisticated information technology-based budget and expenditure management system during its final phase (Phase III 2023–2025). It is noted some government sector units and ADB projects have introduced Microsoft Excel-based accounting tools for maintenance of their accounts.

H.   Responsible Units

Accounting Units

There are 330 accounting units within the government. As per the *Hta Sa*, they are prescribed to follow the procedure laid out in the New Accounting System for Primary Accounting Units of the Government. Each department and/or ministry will consolidate

---

[40]   World Bank. 2014. *Myanmar - Modernization of Public Finance Management Project* (English). Washington, DC; World Bank Group. p. 2.

its accounts based on the accounting system and fiscal reporting prescribed in the *Oo Sa* and submit their accounts to the Treasury Department for consolidation. The Treasury Department then consolidates the accounts as prescribed by the *Sa Ya*. ADB projects based on loan agreement are required to maintain separate accounts and records.

Accounting Staff

MAC is responsible for establishing the curriculum for certified public accountants (CPAs). It has different levels of qualification: (i) CPA (pass), based on passing both Part I and II of the CPA course; and (ii) CPA (full-fledged), based on passing both exams and completing a mandatory 3-year period of apprenticeship. A person receiving the CPA (full-fledged) certificate may register with MAC as a professional accountant and can become a member of the Myanmar Institute of Certified Public Accountants. Note however, that few CPAs work in the government and SEEs compared to the private sector or audit firms.[41] It is an even bigger issue at the state and/or region level. The salary scale in the government sector is a major impediment to attracting qualified staff. One of the challenges identified in a recent World Bank report with regard to budget allocation and execution in the health sector, was the low quantity and capacity of financial management staff, particularly lower down the hierarchy.[42]

The PMU accounting staff are mainly from the relevant ministries, and are under contract in projects and subjected to their limitations.

I.   Fiscal Year

The accounting system and fiscal reporting of Myanmar (*Oo Sa*) specifies that the financial year of the government run from 1 April to 31 March of the following year. The Government of Myanmar has mandated it instead run from 1 October to 30 September, effective October 2018. The financial year of ADB-funded projects are generally aligned with the government fiscal year.

J.   Project Financial Statements

Preparation of Financial Statements

PMUs are required to submit financial statements to ADB and relevant government agencies in accordance with accounting and auditing principles acceptable to ADB.

All government spending units, including PMUs, must submit monthly and fiscal year-end accounts to the relevant directorate, which is in turn responsible for preparation and submission of appropriation accounts to the Auditor General of Myanmar.

---

[41]   Footnote 32, pp. 21–22.
[42]   Footnote 8, p. 19.

Format of Financial Statements to Be Submitted to Government Agencies

The monthly accounts PMUs are required to submit to the directorate must be accompanied by the documents below. The drawing officer is responsible for the completeness and accuracy of these documents.

(i)   Form *Hta Sa*-9 Register for Cash by Detailed Headings
(ii)   Form *Hta Sa*-10 Monthly Cash Statement
(iii) Form *Hta Sa*-11 Monthly Bank Reconciliation Statement
(iv)   Form *Hta Sa*-12 Plus and Minus Account Table for Debt and Deposit Account
(v)   Form *Hta Sa*-6 Cash Balance Certificate

The primary accounting units are to keep their accounts in the forms of *Hta Sa* (directives for keeping accounts for primary accounting units of departments) and send the above monthly accounts to their head offices not later than the 7th of the following month. The departments gather the accounts of the primary accounting units and make a grand total of the whole department in the forms of *Oo Sa* (directives of accounting for departments in compilation and keeping accounts in departments and sending monthly statements to Budget Department). Then the monthly accounts, in the form of *Sa Ya*, with the five parts are to be sent to Treasury Department not later than the 24th of the following month.

Submission of Financial Statements

Projects must submit financial statements to the donor according to the provision in the loan agreement. Although ADB projects allow the executing agency to select the auditor, the Auditor General is responsible for auditing all government entities as per the Auditor General of the Union Law. The relevant line ministry must send a letter to the Auditor General requesting an audit be conducted on a project. The Auditor General sends the audited project financial statements to the relevant line ministry, who relays them to the PMU for forwarding on to ADB.

Deadline for Submission of Financial Statements

The deadline for projects to submit their audited financial statements to ADB is specified in the loan agreement, and is generally 6 months from the end of the fiscal period. PMUs are expected to submit their financial statements to the auditor within 3 months from the end of the fiscal year.

VIII.   Auditing Arrangements

As provisioned by section 242 of the Constitution of the Republic of the Union of Myanmar, 2008, the Auditor General is appointed by the President to audit the Union's accounts of receipt and payment and report to the Union Parliament. The duties of the Auditor General are stated in the Auditor General of the Union Law (Law No. 23 of 2010) are listed in Box 1.

The Auditor General of the Union is assisted by the deputy Auditor General of the Union, appointed by the President, who carries out duties as assigned by the Auditor General.

To conduct audits of the accounts of receipt and payment of regions and/or states, each respective chief minister (with the approval of the region and/or state Parliament and the Union President) appoints a suitable person as region and/or state Auditor General. Region and/or state auditors general are responsible to the Auditor General of the Union, the chief minister of the relevant region and/or state and the President of the Union (through the chief minister).

Auditors general of the Union and region and/or state are assigned audit officers to carry out delegated duties. The duties of the auditors general of regions and/or states are shown in Box 2, while those of audit officers are in Box 3.

Audits are planned quarterly and annually. Any plans prepared by audit offices should be approved by the relevant Auditor General of the region and/or state and Auditor General of the Union. The OAG adopts a semi-annual audit cycle for high-risk ministries.[43] The audit plans are prepared considering the following factors concerning the organizations to be audited:[44]

(i)   the length of time they have unwittingly been left unaudited;
(ii)   any occurrence of problems such as irregularities, fraud, misappropriation, losses, etc.;
(iii)   the importance of their role in national development work; and
(iv)   adequate pre-study in preparation for audit.

The OAG applies generally accepted auditing standards in Myanmar to all audited entities, including core public sector agencies and SEEs.[45] The World Bank Report on Observance of Standards and Codes 2017 noted that that the OAG is modernizing public sector

---

[43]   Country Paper on OAG Myanmar. 2016. p. 4.
[44]   Myanmar Office of the Auditor General, Official website.
[45]   Footnote 32.

Box 1: Duties of the Auditor General of the Union

(a) Submitting the report on auditing the accounts of receipt and payment of the Union as well as implementation of works at least once a year and on the unusual situation from time to time to the session of the Union Parliament, Pyithu Hluttaw or Amyotha Hluttaw;

(b) under the provisions of the Union Budget Law:
   (i) auditing the accounts of receipt and payment of the Union;
   (ii) auditing whether measures have been taken to obtain fully the receipts contained in the budget estimates;
   (iii) auditing whether the sanctioned money contained in the budget estimates are utilized effectively;

(c) auditing whether the set-up and staff strength of relevant government departments and government organizations are appropriate for the responsibilities they have to perform;

(d) auditing whether the appointment of staff of relevant government departments and government organizations are within the sanctioned staff;

(e) auditing whether the set-up and the situation of implementation of works of relevant government departments and government organizations are likely to achieve the original purpose or objective;

(f) auditing whether the union-level organizations, union ministries, government departments, government organizations, and Nay Pyi Taw Council have applied the accounting system that is prescribed in accordance with the existing financial regulations;

(g) auditing whether the projects and implementation of works of the union-level organizations, union ministries, government departments, government organizations and Nay Pyi Taw Council are actually effective for the public;

(h) (i) auditing whether there is precise, accurate, systematic maintenance and effective utilization in taking over and using state-owned assets, cooperative-owned assets, and public-owned assets;
   (ii) auditing whether ownerless assets, confiscated assets, assets that are taken over as public-owned by notification and assets legally relinquished by the owner are officially recorded in the accounts, maintained, utilized systematically, and in case of necessity, systematically disposed and transferred;

(i) in respect of manufacturing, trading and services:
   (i) auditing the accounts of manufacturing, trading, and services;
   (ii) auditing the quantity and standards of products and services;
   (iii) auditing whether there are wastages, leakages, damages, losses, and misappropriation in implementing projects;
   (iv) comparing and auditing the cost and effectiveness;
   (v) auditing supervision over an organization or the way the organization works, performing work under effective operational controls, improvement in economic efficiency, social and cultural impact, systematic work, performance of staff is free from corruption, and beneficial utilization of funds and properties;

(j) presenting findings to the relevant organizations after auditing as the case may be if the President of the Union, speaker of the Union Parliament, speaker of the Pyithu Hluttaw, or speaker of the Amyotha Hluttaw or any union-level organization, any union ministry or Nay Pyi Taw Council request to audit any of its activities;

(k) supervising the Myanmar Accountancy Council and the Myanmar Institute of Certified Public Accountants, and providing necessary guidance;

(l) determining and supervising the duties, ethics, and rights of the certified public accountant and the practicing accountant in accordance with the law;

(m) auditing, if necessary, the accounts of private business that have been audited by the certified public accountant and the practicing accountant relating to taxes to be paid to the Union;

(n) submitting necessary bill relating to the auditing works to the Union Parliament;

(o) reporting his performance and findings to the President of the Union and the Union Parliament simultaneously;

continued on next page

Box 1 continued

(p) submitting the report to the Union Parliament if the Union Parliament assigns him to audit the implementation of works of the union-level organizations, union ministries, government departments, government organizations, and Nay Pyi Taw Council;

(q) auditing the accounts of receipt and payment relating to debt, deposits, and suspense which are operated in conjunction with the Union Budget at union-level organizations, union ministries, government departments, government organizations, and Nay Pyi Taw Council, and checking whether the responsible persons systematically control and effectively supervise such receipts and payments;

(r) auditing whether the internal audit teams have been formed at the organizations, which will be audited according to the law, and whether such teams carry out their activities in accordance with the work programs, orders, directives, and procedures determined by the relevant ministries and organizations;

(s) in auditing the organizations or works that will be audited according to the law, sending the findings regarding the matters considered to require legal actions to the head of the relevant organizations and to the member of its union-level organization and that of its region or state-level organization;

(t) in auditing any organization or work, if it is considered to be stopped and prevented forthwith, the wastages, leakages, damages, losses, and misappropriation are currently occurring in such organization or worksite;

    (i) informing immediately to the head of the relevant organizations and the member of its union-level organization and that of its region- or state-level organization;

    (ii) reporting to the union government and relevant region or state government, if the head of the relevant organizations does not take any action;

(u) (i) entering and auditing premises and buildings of the organizations, offices, worksites, and factories that will be audited according to the law;

    (ii) requesting and auditing projects, plans, operation systems, contracts, list of personnel, cash accounts, asset accounts, reports, books of account, vouchers, and other documents maintained in the organizations, offices, worksites, and factories that will be audited according to the law;

    (iii) in requesting the documents mentioned in subsection (ii), causing the relevant organizations to send the original or copy of them or by the electronic system;

    (iv) maintaining the evidential properties, documents, recorded disks, and electronic records that are found regarding auditing as exhibits;

    (v) interviewing relevant persons for the purpose of auditing and obtaining statements;

    (vi) obtaining the help of skilled staff according to the work or timeframe with the approval of the relevant organization for auditing, if necessary;

(v) auditing the accounts relating to the other financial matters of government departments and government organizations, if necessary;

(w) auditing the works and accounts of joint ventures operating with the government that are granted benefits by various types of agreements and various systems utilizing state-owned water, land, air, and resources, if necessary;

(x) auditing whether law, regulations, bylaws, and procedures are compiled in regard to loans borrowed from this country or abroad, loans disbursed to this country or abroad, interest paid and interest received on loans;

(y) auditing whether moneys and assets receivable and moneys and assets payable are disclosed completely and accurately and whether accounts are cleared in accordance with the prescriptions;

(z) performing other duties assigned by the President of the Union in accordance with the law;

(aa) performing other duties stipulated under any existing law."

Source: Government of Myanmar. 2018. Auditor General of the Union Law No. 23 of 2010 (with Amending Law No. 3 of 2013, Amending Law No. 43 of 2014 and Amending Law 2018).

Box 2: Duties of the Auditor General of the Region or State

The Auditor General of the region or state is responsible for the following:

(a) submitting the report on auditing related to the accounts of receipt and payment of the region and state as well as of the implementation of works at least once a year and on the unusual situation from time to time to the session of the relevant region or state hluttaw;

(b) according to the provisions contained in the budget law of the relevant region or state:
   (i) auditing the accounts of the receipt and payment of the region or state;
   (ii) auditing whether or not measures have been taken to obtain fully the receipts contained in the budget estimates;
   (iii) auditing whether or not the sanctioned money contained in the budget estimates are utilized effectively;

(c) auditing whether the implementation of works of the relevant region- or state-level organizations, region or state ministries, government departments, or government organizations are actually effective for the public;

(d) submitting the report on theirperformance and findings to the chief minister of the region or state and to the region or state hluttaw simultaneously;

(e) performing other duties assigned by the Auditor General of the union or the chief minister of the relevant region or state in accord with law;

(f) submitting the report to the region or state hluttaw if the region or state hluttaw assigns him to audit the implementation of work of the relevant region- or state-level organizations, government departments, and government organizations;

(g) auditing the accounts relating to the other financial matters of the government departments and government organizations of the region or state, if necessary;

(h) auditing, if necessary and assigned, the works and accounts of joint ventures operating with the relevant region or state government, which are granted benefits by various types of agreements and various systems utilizing state-owned water, land, air, and resources;

(i) auditing the accounts of receipt and payment relating to debt, deposits, and suspense which are operated in conjunction with the region or state budget and assigning audit officers to check whether the responsible persons systematically control and effectively supervise such receipts and payments;

(j) auditing whether moneys and assets receivable and moneys and assets payable are disclosed completely and accurately, and whether accounts are cleared in accordance with the prescriptions; and

(k) performing other duties stipulated under any existing law.

Source: Government of Myanmar. 2018. Auditor General of the Union Law No. 23 of 2010 (with Amending Law No. 3 of 2013, Amending Law No. 43 of 2014 and Amending Law 2018).

---

auditing standards, working toward compliance with level four financial audit guidelines (international standards of supreme audit institutions) with capacity building assistance from development partners.

The OAG predominantly performs financial and compliance audits and some performance audits.[46] Discussions with OAG officials indicated that the office is considering the introduction of risk-based audits. The OAG is mandated to conduct

---

[46]   World Bank. 2013. *Republic of the Union of Myanmar - Public financial management performance report* (Vol. 2): Full report (English). Washington, DC: World Bank. Section 330.

Box 3: Duties of the Audit Officers

Under the provisions contained in the union budget law and budget law of the relevant region or state, audit officers are responsible for:

(a) auditing the accounts of the receipt and payment of its relevant government departments and government organizations;

    (i) auditing whether or not measures have been taken to obtain fully the receipts of its relevant government departments and government organizations;

    (ii) auditing whether or not the sanctioned money is utilized effectively by its relevant government departments and government organizations;

    (iii) auditing whether the implementation of works of the relevant organizations are actually effective for the public;

(b) performing other duties assigned by the Auditor General of the union or Auditor General of the region or state in accord with law;

(c) (i) submitting reports on his performance to the Auditor General of the region or state if he is an audit officer of the self-administered division or self-administered zone and district audit officer;

    (ii) submitting reports on his performances to the Auditor General of the region or state through the audit officer of the relevant self-administered division or self-administered zone or district audit officer if they are a township audit officer; and.

(d) auditing the accounts of receipt and payments relating to debt, deposit, suspense which are operated in conjunction with the Region or State Budget and checking whether the responsible person systematically controls and effectively supervises such receipts and payments.

Source: Government of Myanmar. Auditor General of the Union Law No. 23 of 2010 (with Amending Law No. 3 of 2013, Amending Law No. 43 of 2014 and Amending Law 2018.)

---

audits for around 170 government units, including ministries, departments, agencies, SEEs, and projects. It carries out approximately 15,000 audits per year with a staff of over 6,000. It is noted that while the OAG is responsible for auditing all public funds, it needs more capacity in relation to auditing foreign-funded projects. Additionally, due to arising job opportunities in the private sector with higher salaries, many auditors have resigned and the current capacity of OAG requires strengthening. ADB's "Enhancing Roles of Supreme Audit Institutions in Selected Association of Southeast Asian Nations Countries" project targets this issue.[47] With regard to audits conducted by OAG for SEEs, the World Bank's *Report on Observance of Standards and Codes* (2017) noted that some SEEs are financial institutions and consideration should be given to the current capacity of the OAG to perform quality audits for them.[48]

Organizations being audited by OAG are required to submit their financial statements for audit within 3 months from the end of the fiscal year. As this mandate is not stated officially in any law, steps are being taken to legally define the deadlines. The OAG takes at least 3 months to release audit reports.

---

[47] Asian Development Bank. 2016. *Enhancing Roles of Supreme Audit Institutions in Selected Association of Southeast Asian Nations Countries.* Manila.

[48] Footnote 32, Section 147.

The findings from different audit offices are consecutively gathered and are included in the Auditor General's report. Before finalizing the report, the audit team led by the deputy Auditor General discusses its findings with the audited organization.[49] In the event fraud or misappropriations are discovered, an interim audit report is issued without completing the entire audit.[50] The OAG submits its audit reports to the President and the Parliament twice a year.

The audited organizations are required to provide responses to the audit findings stated in the audit report within a reasonable period of time after the reports have been issued. The time limit within which they are required to respond is communicated when the reports are sent to them. The organizations are expected to take necessary actions, based on the audit points and observations highlighted by the OAG.[51]

A.   Auditing Requirements

The audit requirements for donor-funded projects are established in the respective grant and/or loan agreement between the government and the development partner. An external audit terms of reference is signed once the project grant and/or loan agreement is signed. The executing agency is required to appoint an auditor for their projects that is acceptable to the development partner. The OAG is selected for this purpose.

Through the respective minister, projects submit a letter and project financial statements at year-end to the OAG requesting an audit. Projects are required to prepare their financial statements according to ADB guidelines, or in the event no specifications are given, according to national financial regulations. The executing agency needs to submit the project annual financial statements to OAG within 3 months from the end of the fiscal year.

The OAG applies generally accepted auditing standards to project financial statements and submits audit reports in Myanmarese to the executing agency, with a copy to the respective PMU, within 3 months from receipt of the statements. The PMU is required to submit the English translation of the audit report to ADB within 6 months from the completion of the fiscal year. The report contains the audited financial statements and the auditor's opinion on the statements. The report also includes a management letter noting the weaknesses identified in the internal controls, and additional auditor's opinions on the use of loan proceeds and compliance with financial covenants, where applicable.[52] During the fiscal year 2017, OAG audited 48 foreign-funded projects, of which 5 were from ADB.[53]

---

[49]   Country Paper on OAG Myanmar. 2016. p. 4. - http://164.115.40.103/inter_asosai/symposium/content.php?article+48.

[50]   Myanmar Office of the Auditor General, Official website.

[51]   Footnote 52.

[52]   ADB. 2015. Financial Reporting and Auditing of Loan- and Grant-Financed Projects. Project Administration Instructions. PAI 5.07. Manila.

[53]   Discussion with the officials of Office of the Auditor General during field mission in July 2017.

B.   Resolution of Problems Raised in External Audit Reports

Findings raised in the project audit reports are included in the executing agency's audit reports, which are submitted to the PAC for review. The executing agencies are generally given 1 month to provide their response to the OAG on the issues raised. Responses related are prepared by the respective PMU and submitted to the executing agency for inclusion in the response to the OAG.

IX.   Summary of Risks and Issues, and Proposed Mitigating Actions and Improvements

Table 3 summarizes the risks and issues in the Myanmar's financial management systems that may affect project implementation. These risks and issues should be considered by project officers and mission leaders when designing financial management arrangements and conducting financial management and risk assessments. Some useful references and suggested readings are provided in the Appendix 5.

Table 3: Common Issues, Problems, and Suggestions for Mitigating or Avoiding Risks

Observation	Recommendation
Project Appraisal Projects are not systematically appraised and prioritized. Although the National Development Plan and sector strategies outline the overall development plans of the government, the selection of projects are not based on systematic appraisal before entering the budget.	It is noted some progress has been made in developing appraisal guidelines. However, as critical gaps still remain in the process, it is recommended to establish regulation and improve appraisal capacity of relevant staff for strategic project selection.
Reporting Standards Government sector units adapt a single-entry, modified cash-based accounting system based on generally accepted accounting principles. However, it is not in compliance with international standards.	As the government has shown intent to be in compliant with international accounting standards with reporting aligned with International Public Sector Accounting Standards, ADB could consider supporting this effort.
Reporting System The government accounting system is paper-based with compilation of budget execution reports and financial statements being almost entirely manual. This leads to delays in compilation of reports, timely analysis of data, and a lack of consolidated picture of Myanmar's financial position.	The longer term strategy of the government targets computerization of the accounting system in the Public Financial Management System Reformation Strategy, 2013–2025. The World Bank's Modernization of Public Finance Management Project is supporting the government in the computerization of the accounting and reporting function on a progressive basis. ADB may consider supporting these efforts.

continued on next page

Table 3 continued

Observation	Recommendation
Accounting Staff There are limited numbers of certified public accountants working in the government. Lack of capacity of accounting staff is also a challenge, particularly lower down the structure.	ADB may consider supporting the capacity building of government accounting staff.
Internal Controls Due to lack of standard operating guidelines, spending agencies develop their own detailed procedures and systems on matters that should be subjected to government-wide standards. Therefore, processes followed by spending bodies may not meet minimum procedural controls.	ADB may consider supporting developing standard operating procedures for critical spending dimensions.
Internal Audit Weak internal control and the lack of an internal audit function are evident in many spending bodies. Although internal audit units are required in all large-scale public bodies, it is not available in practice.	Guidelines and capacity should be put in place to ensure implementation of internal audit functions across government entities.
External Audit While efforts are being taken to improve OAG functions, requirement for capacity to handle complex audits, such as financial institutions and risk-based audit methodologies, will be a challenge.	Support for capacity building of OAG staff, especially for complex audits. Another option would be outsourcing audits, which is being supported by ADB's ongoing technical assistance.

ADB = Asian Development Bank, OAG = Office of the Auditor General.

Source: Asian Development Bank.

X. Confirmation and/or Endorsement by Government Stakeholders

The Republic of the Union of Myanmar
Ministry of Investment and Foreign Economic Relations
Foreign Economic Relations Department

No. 68 / 70 / 01 (0830 / 2020)
Dated. 10th March   2020

Mr. Newin Sinsiri
Country Director
Myanmar Resident Mission
Asian Development Bank
Tel: (+95) 678106280–6286
Fax: (+95) 678106287

Dear Mr. Newin Sinsiri,

Subject: **Report on the Public Financial Management Systems**

With reference to your letter dated 23rd October 2019, we have no-objection to the publication of Report on the Public Financial Management Systems of Myanmar.

Yours Sincerely,

for Director General,
(Moh Moh Naing – Director)

cc :   Budget Department, Ministry of Planning, Finance and Industry
        Treasury Department, Ministry of Planning, Finance and Industry
        Project Appraisal and Progress Reporting Department, Ministry of Planning, Finance and Industry
        Office of Auditor General
        Central Bank of Myanmar

XI. Works Cited

Asian Development Bank. 2017. *Loan Disbursement Handbook*. Manila: Asian Development Bank.

Asian Development Bank. 2016. *Enhancing Roles of Supreme Audit Institutions in Selected Association of Southeast Asian Nations Countries*. Manila.

Asian Development Bank. 2015. Financial Reporting and Auditing of Loan- and Grant-Financed Projects. Project Administration Instructions. PAI 5.07. Manila

2016. Country Paper on OAG Myanmar. p. 4.

FERD Website. https://www.mopf.gov.mm/en/page/planning/foreign-economic-relations-ferd/171.

Government of Myanmar. 2018a. *Development Assistance Policy*. January 2018.

Government of Myanmar. 2018b. *Myanmar Sustainable Development Plan 2018–2030*. p. 39.

Government of Myanmar. 2018c. Myanmar Office of the Auditor General. Official website. https://www.oagmac.gov.mm/ (accessed 4 January 2020).

Government of Myanmar. 2018d. *Auditor General of the Union Law No. 23 of 2010* (with Amending Law No. 3 of 2013, Amending Law No. 43 of 2014 and Amending Law 2018).

Government of Myanmar. 2017. *Citizen's Budget 2017–2018 Fiscal Year Budget Information*. Ministry of Planning and Finance.

Government of Myanmar. 2017 Ministry of Planning and Finance – Official website. https://www.mopf.gov.mm/en.

Government of Myanmar. 2016. *Myanmar Public Debt Management Law, 2016*. Chapter II, section 3.

Government of Myanmar. 2013. *Central Bank of Myanmar Law. No. 16*. Unofficial Translation. http://www.asianlii.org/mm/legis/laws/cbomlhln162013505.pdf (accessed 4 January 2020).

Government of Myanmar. 2008. *The Constitution of the Republic of the Myanmar 2008.* Section 195.

PwC. 2014. *Myanmar Business Guide: Accounting and Auditing Regulations in Myanmar.* p. 22.

SS Oo. 2016. *Fiscal Management Reform in Myanmar (Lessons Drawn from Japanese Experiences).* Paper by Visiting Scholar from the Policy Research Institute, Ministry of Finance, Japan.

World Bank Group. 2017. *Myanmar Public Expenditure Review 2017: Fiscal Space for Economic Growth.* Yangon: World Bank. p. 30.

World Bank. 2017. *Myanmar - Report on Observance of Standards and Codes (ROSC): accounting and auditing module* (English). Washington, DC: World Bank Group. p. 28.

World Bank. 2014. Myanmar - Modernization of Public Finance Management Project (English). Washington, DC: World Bank Group. p. 2.

World Bank. 2013. *Republic of the Union of Myanmar - Public financial management performance report (Vol. 2).* Washington, DC: World Bank. p. 66.

Z. Oo et al. 2015. *Fiscal Management in Myanmar. ADB Economics Working Paper Series No. 434.* Manila: Asian Development Bank.

Appendix 1
Timeline for Preparing Budget Estimates of the Union (Fiscal Year from 1 October to 30 September)

No.	Particular	Timeline
1	Issuing budget calendar with revenue and expenditure ceiling to union-level organizations by the Ministry of Planning and Finance	3rd week of February
2	Sending from union-level organizations to Budget Department	3rd week of March
3	Analyzing by Budget Department, Equipment Control Committee, Coordination and Scrutiny Committee of Construction Works and Planning Department, and compiling	3rd week of March – 2nd week of April
4	Scrutinizing by the Deputy Minister of Planning and Finance and resending from the union-level organization to the Budget Department after scrutinizing by the Deputy Minister	3rd week of April – 1st week of May
5	Scrutinizing by the Minister of Planning and Finance and resending from the union-level organization to the Budget Department after scrutinizing by the Union Minister	2nd week of May – 3rd week of May
6	Scrutinizing by Vice-President and resending to Budget Department after scrutinizing by Vice-President and compilation	4th week of May – 1st week of June
7	Submitting to Economic Committee	2nd week of June
8	Submitting to Financial Commission	3rd week of June
9	Submitting to the Cabinet Meeting	3rd week of June
10	Requesting Budget Proposal of union-level organizations by Budget Department to submit to the Union Parliament and resending budget proposal of union-level organizations to Budget Department	4th week of June – 1st week of July
11	Sending budget proposal of union-level organizations and the Union Budget Bill by the union government to the Union Parliament	1st week of July
12	Submitting the union budget bill to the Union Parliament by union Minister of Planning and Finance on behalf of the union government	Before 15 July
13	Approving by the Union Parliament	3rd week of September
14	Signing on the union budget law by the President	Before end of September

Source: Government of Myanmar. Ministry of Planning and Finance. Budget Department.

Appendix 2
Timeline for Preparing Budget Estimates for the Supplementary Budget of the Union (Fiscal Year from 1 October to 30 September)

No.	Particular	Timeline
1	Issuing Supplementary Budget Calendar to union-level organizations	1st week of February
2	Sending from union-level organizations to Budget Department	2nd week of February
3	Analyzing and compiling by Budget Department	3rd week of February – 1st week of March
4	Scrutinizing by Deputy Minister of Planning and Finance and resending from the union-level organization to the Budget Department after scrutinized by the Deputy Minister and compilation	1st week of March – 3rd week of March
5	Scrutinizing by the Union Minister of Planning and Finance and resending from the union-level Organization to the Budget Department after scrutinizing by the Union Minister	3rd week of March – 4th week of March
6	Scrutinizing by Vice-President and resending from union-level organizations to Budget Department after scrutinized by Vice-President and compiling	4th week of March – 1st week of April
7	Submitting to Economic Committee	2nd week of April
8	Submitting to Financial Commission	2nd week of April
9	Submitting to the Cabinet	2nd week of April
10	Requesting Supplementary Budget Proposal of union-level organizations by Budget Department to submit to the Union Parliament and resending the Budget Proposal by union-level organizations to Budget Department	2nd week of April – 3rd week of April
11	Sending Supplementary Budget Proposal of union-level organizations and the Supplementary Appropriation Bill by the Union Government to the Union Parliament	3rd week of April
12	Submitting the Union Supplementary Appropriation Bill to the Union Parliament by Union Minister of Planning and Finance on behalf of the Union Government	Before 30 April
13	Approving by the Union Parliament	3rd week of September
14	Signing of the Union Budget Law by the President	Before end of September

Source: Government of Myanmar. Ministry of Planning and Finance. Budget Department.

Appendix 3
Timeline for Preparing Budget Estimates of Regions and/or States

No.	Particular	Timeline
1	Discussion between Union Ministry of Planning and Finance and Ministers of States and Regions Ministry of Planning and Finance concerned with subsidies amount	1st week of January
2	Sending budget calendar to State and Region from Ministry of Planning and Finance	1st week of January
3	Announcing subsidies amount to state and region (announcing subsidies ceiling from union cabinet)	3rd week of January
4	Sending budget proposals from region and/or state-level organizations to respective state and/or region Budget Departments	2nd week of February
5	Sending budget proposals to Budget Department (headquarters)	4th week of April
6	Scrutinizing by Ministry of Planning and Finance	1st week or 2nd week of May
7	Scrutinizing by Vice-President	3rd week or 4th week of May
8	Financial commission meeting	3rd week of June
9	Submitting to Union Parliament	Before 15 July
10	Approving of subsidies by Union Parliament	During September
11	Announcing the subsidies amount approved by Union Parliament	During September
12	Submitting to region and/or state hluttaw	During September
13	Approving by region and/or state chief minister	End of September

Source: Government of Myanmar. Ministry of Planning and Finance. Budget Department.

Appendix 4
Administrative Structure
of the Government

Historically Myanmar's fiscal, administrative, and political structures have been highly centralized. However, the 2008 Constitution formally established subnational governments (states and regions), each with a legislature, judiciary, and executive. The Government of Myanmar is organized into the Union (i.e., central government) and the subnational government with 7 states, 7 regions, and 1 union territory. The states and regions are formed with districts, self-administered zones, and self-administered divisions. The townships in a self-administered zone are organized as self-administered zones whereas townships in a self-administered division are organized as districts and such districts are organized as self-administered divisions. If there are self-administered zones or self-administered divisions in a region or a state, those self-administered divisions, self-administered zones, and districts are organized as regions or states. Figure 6 illustrates how the union is constituted.

Figure: Administrative Structure of Myanmar

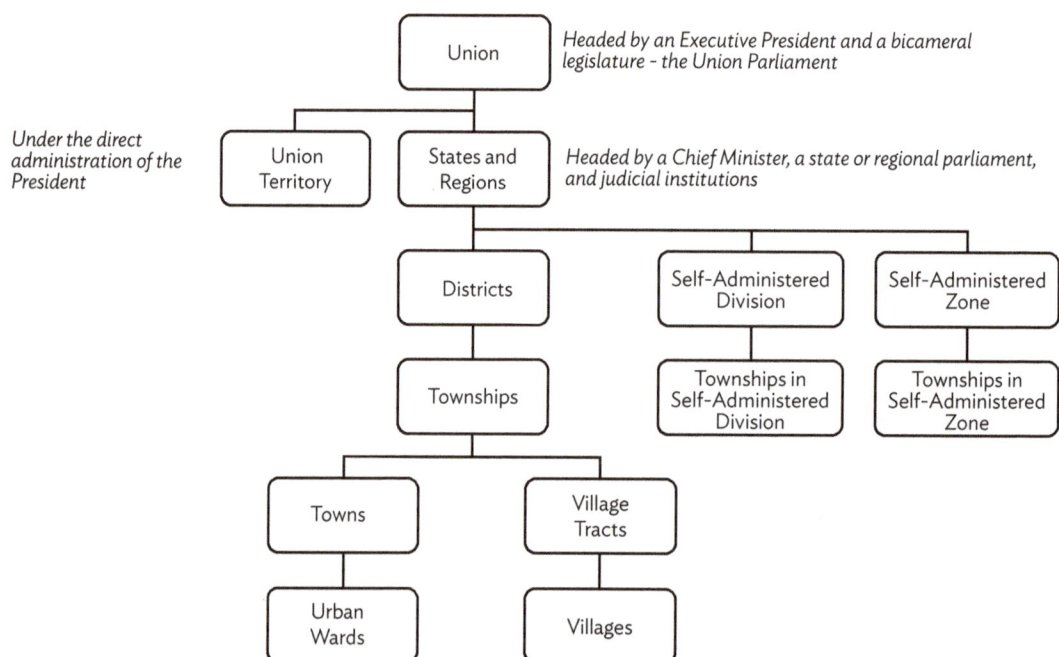

Source: Asian Development Bank.

Appendix 5
Useful References
and Suggested Reading

Government Institutions Official Websites

Central Bank of Myanmar. http://www.cbm.gov.mm.

Ministry of Planning and Finance. http://www.mof.gov.mm/en/content/about-us.

Ministry of Planning and Finance, Budget Department. http://www.mof.gov.mm/en/content/budget-department.

Office of the Auditor General. http://www.oagmac.gov.mm/content/audit-operation.

Acts and Regulations

Central Bank of Myanmar Law–Pyidaungsu Hluttaw Law No. 16/2013 (Unofficial translation).

Public Debt Management Law–Pyidaungsu Hluttaw Law No. 2/2016.

The Auditor General of the Union Law–The State Peace and Development Council Law No. 23/2010.

The Constitution of the Republic of the Myanmar 2008.

The Myanmar Accountancy Council Law–The Pyidaungsu Hluttaw Law No. 31/2015.

The Union Budget Law–The Pyidaungsu Hluttaw Law No. 20/2015.

Asian Development Bank Reports and Documents

Asian Development Bank. 2016. *Auditor's Report on the Activities and Accounts of Greater Mekong Subregion: Capacity Building for HIV/AIDS Prevention the JFRR Project for the period of 4 June 2014 to 31 March 2016*. Manila: Asian Development Bank.

Asian Development Bank. Project Data Sheet - Enhancing Roles of Supreme Audit Institutions in Selected Association of Southeast Asian Nations Countries. Manila: Asian Development Bank.

Other Sources

IFRS. 2019. Myanmar. http://www.ifrs.org/use-around-the-world/use-of-ifrs-standards-by-jurisdiction/myanmar. Updated: 17 April 2019. Accessed: 2 April 2020. London: IFRS.

Mohinga. Foreign Economic Relations Department. Accessed: 2 April 2020. https://mohinga.info/en/profiles/donor/FERD-MM Nay Pyi Taw, Myanmar: Mohinga.

Country Paper on OAG Myanmar. 2016.

San San Oo. 2016. *Fiscal Management Reform in Myanmar (Lessons Drawn from Japanese Experiences)*. Visiting Scholar, Policy Research Institute. Tokyo: Ministry of Finance.

World Bank. 2014. *Project Appraisal Document, Modernization of Public Financial Management Project*. Report No. PAD925. 25 February 2014. Washington, DC: World Bank.

World Bank. 2017. *Report on Observance of Standards and Codes (ROSC), Accounting and Auditing Module – Myanmar.* June 2017. Washington, DC: World Bank.

World Bank. 2017. *Myanmar Public Expenditure Review – Fiscal Space for Economic Growth.* Washington, DC: World Bank.

World Bank. 2013. *Republic of the Union of Myanmar – Public Finance Management Performance Report – Myanmar.* May 2013. Washington, DC: World Bank.

www.ingramcontent.com/pod-product-compliance
Lightning Source LLC
Chambersburg PA
CBHW040146200326
41519CB00035B/7610